J331.7 84-262
W24
Wandro
  My Daddy is a Nurse

DATE DUE			
AUG 16 '84			
AUG 30 '84			
OCT 4 '84			
OCT 18 1984			
NOV 22 1984			
JAN 31 85			
MAY 26 1988			
APR 13 1989			
MAY 4 1989			
SEP 27 1990			

Chanute Public Library
Chanute, Kansas 66720

My Daddy is a Nurse

My Daddy is a Nurse

by Mark Wandro, R.N.
and Joani Blank
Illustrated by Irene Trivas

▲
▲▼
Addison-Wesley

Text Copyright © 1981 by Mark Wandro and Joani Blank
Illustrations Copyright © 1981 by Irene Trivas
All Rights Reserved
Addison-Wesley Publishing Company, Inc.
Reading, Massachusetts 01867
Printed in the United States of America

ABCDEFGHIJK-WZ-8987654321

CHANUTE PUBLIC LIBRARY
102 S. Lincoln
CHANUTE, KS 66720

Library of Congress Cataloging in Publication Data

Wandro, Mark.
  My daddy is a nurse.

  Summary: Describes the work of men with ten occupations traditionally reserved for women: nurse, flight attendant, homemaker, dental hygienist, weaver, children's librarian, telephone operator, ballet dancer, office worker, and preschool teacher.
  1. Occupations—Pictorial works—Juvenile literature.
  2. Employment of men—Pictorial works—Juvenile literature. [1. Occupations] I. Blank, Joani,
  II. Trivas, Irene. III. Title.
  HF5381.2.W35   331.7'02'024041   81-3438
  ISBN 0-201-08323-X   AACR2

For Amika

Some daddies drive trucks.

Some daddies are doctors.

Some daddies work in factories.

Some daddies are storekeepers.

Some daddies build houses.

BUT NOT MY DADDY.

My daddy works in a very big hospital. He works very hard. He is not a doctor; he is a nurse. He has a stethoscope and a thermometer, and he takes care of people who are sick.

He teaches them how to stay well, too.

This daddy is a flight attendant. He works on a big airplane that flies across the country three times a week. He knows all about the safety rules for the plane. He has toys and games for the children, and he brings food and drinks to everybody. He knows a lot about all the different places the people are going to.

This daddy is a preschool teacher. Every morning he is at school when the children get there. They have fun learning about numbers and colors and the letters of the alphabet. He also knows lots of songs and games.
When it is sunny, he takes everyone for a walk to the park or to the library.

This daddy is a dental hygienist. He works in a dentist's office. People who come to have their teeth cleaned and checked sit in his special chair that goes up and down like a slow elevator. He uses an electric toothbrush that spins around very fast and makes a whirring sound. He also has a big bright light and a tiny mirror so he can see all around inside people's mouths where it is usually very dark.

This daddy is a weaver. The place where he works is called a studio. He sits at his loom and makes beautiful cloth. He knows how to put fancy designs into the weaving. Sometimes he takes the things he makes to arts and crafts shows.

Right now he is working on a huge wall hanging.

This daddy is a librarian. He helps children find the books they want to read. There are hundreds of books in his library but he can almost always find the right one. His favorite day is Thursday because that is when a lot of kids come to the library for story hour.

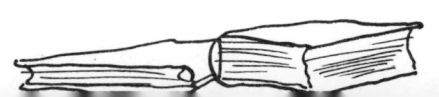

This daddy is a telephone operator. He usually works in the evening so he can take his kids to school almost every day and give them their lunch too. At work he wears a neat headset so he can hear all the people calling him up and still use both of his hands to push buttons. Sometimes he helps people call their friends all around the world.

This daddy is a ballet dancer. He practices four or five hours every day. He is as strong as a basketball or football player. He can lift his partners high in the air, and he never drops them. He can leap all the way across the stage in only three or four steps. When he gets ready for a performance, he wears a handsome costume and dancing shoes.

This daddy is an office worker. He has his own desk and a telephone and a typewriter. He can type very fast without even looking at the typewriter. He stops to answer the telephone when it rings. He puts every important paper in exactly the right place in the file near his desk.

This daddy is a homemaker. He doesn't work in a factory or an office or a hospital or a studio. But he has a lot of work to do. He cleans the house and cooks the meals and spends a lot of time with the baby. His daughter, Jessie, really likes to go shopping after school with her dad and her baby brother.

What does your daddy do?